Complete Slavonic Dances
for Piano Four Hands

ANTONÍN DVOŘÁK

From the Czech Complete-Works Edition

DOVER PUBLICATIONS, INC., *New York*

This Dover edition, first published in 1992, is a republication of Series V, Volume 5: *Slovanské Tance (Slavonic Dances)* from *Souborné Vydání děl Antonína Dvořáka (Complete Edition of Antonín Dvořák's Works)*, published by Společnost Antonína Dvořáka, Státní Nakladatelství Krásné Literatury, Hudby a Umění, Prague, 1955. The Czech and French versions of the editorial notes have been omitted.

We are grateful to the library of the Aaron Copland School of Music, Queens College, for the loan of the score for reproduction.

Manufactured in the United States of America
Dover Publications, Inc., 31 East 2nd Street, Mineola, N.Y. 11501

Library of Congress Cataloging-in-Publication Data

Dvořák, Antonín. 1841–1904.
   [Slovanské tance, op. 46]
   Complete Slavonic dances : for piano four hands : from the Czech complete-works edition / Antonín Dvořák.
       p.   of music.
   Reprint. Originally published: Prague : Artia, 1955. (Souborné vydání děl Antonína Dvořáka. Series 5 : v. 5).
   Contents: Op. 46 (1878) — Op. 72 (1886).
   ISBN 0-486-27019-X
   1. Piano music (4 hands). 2. Dance music — Czechoslovakia. I. Dvořák, Antonín, 1841–1904. Slovanské tance, op. 72. 1992. II. Title. III. Title: Slavonic dances.
M201.D9 op. 46 1992   91-36242
                                                  CIP
                                                     M

Contents

Editorial Notes

SLAVONIC DANCES

OP. 46

(Piano duet)

Critical edition based on original sources and prepared for the press by the Editing Board for the Works of Antonín Dvořák: Otakar Šourek, Chairman - Jan Hanuš, Chief Editor - František Bartoš - Dr Jiří Berkovec - Dr Antonín Čubr - Ladislav Láska - Antonín Pokorný - Karel Šolc.

TWO SERIES OF "SLAVONIC DANCES", each of them consisting of eight numbers, belong to the most individual, personal, nationally most characteristic and most famous works of *Antonín Dvořák* (September 8th 1841—May 1st 1904). They were not written successively: the second series (op. 72) followed the first (op. 46) after an interval of eight years. Both series differ substantially in many aspects but both are typically characteristic of Dvořák not only in construction but also in power of effect and vitality, and both originated in the same way as they were written in response to a suggestion of Fritz Simrock, the proprietor of the big publishing house N. Simrock in Berlin. Both were first composed for the piano duet, appeared only later in the full glamour of colourful orchestration and spread quickly through the world where time has not only preserved but even heightened their original success.

Simrock asked Dvořák for the first series of "Slavonic Dances" immediately after Johannes Brahms had acquainted him with Dvořák's "Moravian Duets", as he realised the importance of the interest caused by their publication and understood the exceedingly national characteristics of the talent of the hitherto unknown Czech composer. He suggested to Dvořák to create a series of "Slavonic Dances" for piano duet in a style similar to that which had recently proved so successful in the case of Brahms' "Hungarian Dances".

Dvořák, pleased at the publisher's interest that seemed to open all the world for him, responded to this stimulus very enthusiastically and immediately: he interrupted his work on the cycle of "Slavonic Rhapsodies" and the following day after having finished the first of them, i. e. March 18th 1878, he began the manuscript of the eight "Slavonic Dances" op. 46, the third of which (in A flat major) he finished on April 4th, the fourth on April 9th and the last, eighth, on May 7th 1878 (the manuscript, which is in the possession of the composer's heirs, does not include any other dates). The undated sketch of these dances (in the possession of Prof. Václav Talich) must have been the result of only a few moments and its appearance also testifies to the wonderful spontaneity with which these dances were created: hastily and evidently in a hurry, in order that the pen could catch up with the quickly arising ideas, it sketches only the main melodic ideas of each dance with only a few isolated hints such as *"melody in the bass"*, or *"left hand figuration"*, or statements of the respective basic harmony.

When considering the "Slavonic Dances" it is important to realise that Dvořák used only the basic idea of the suggestion made to him by the publisher: to create artistic stylisation of characteristic Slavonic dances. Unlike Brahms in his "Hungarian Dances", Dvořák did not use as his starting point the music of original folk dance songs but only made use of their rhythms as their most characteristic and expressive element, otherwise creating his dances from a musical material which was his own and new. In this first series of "Slavonic Dances" — with the exception of the second which is a typical Dvořák stylisation of the Ukrainean Dumka — he chose for this purpose characteristic types of Czech dances, viz. Furiant (No. 1. and 8.), Polka (No. 3.), Sousedská (Neighbours' Dance — No. 4. and 6.) and Skočná (Jump Dance — No. 5. and 7.) — i. e. mostly merry dances, expressing a healthy joy of life. (It should be noted that this numbering of the dances which has also been preserved in the present edition, is in accordance with the numbering used in the composer's sketches and the score, whereas in Simrock's edition of the piano duet version the places of the third and sixth dance were changed.)

The first series of the "Slavonic Dances" was published in the original piano duet version by Simrock as early as 1878. The relation of our new edition to this first print is discussed in detail in the Editors' Notes following the last page of music.

Otakar Šourek

Translated by Dr. L. Dorůžka

EDITORS' NOTES

SOURCES:

a) The manuscript of the original piano version of the first series of "Slavonic Dances", in the possession of the composer's family, is written quite carelessly, sometimes even hardly legibly, in the form of a score ("secondo" written right under the "primo") on 20 stave music paper 243 : 308 mm in size (after the sheets have been cut by the book-binder), and is bound in one volume with the manuscript of the cycle "From the Bohemian Forest". The original title page has been glued over with another sheet of music paper, smaller in size, on which Dvořák hastily sketched — but probably only some time later — in ink: "*Slovanské tance | pro piano | na 4 ruce | složil | Antonín Dvořák | op. 46*" (Slavonic Dances / for piano / duet / composed / by Antonín Dvořák / op. 46). Before the fifth dance there is another title page, bearing the same inscription as the first, with the words "*sešit II.*" ("Book II.") added after the first line and "*Číslo* [No.] *5 Allegro vivace | 6 Allegretto scherzando | 7 Allegro | 8 Furiant*" after the opus number; in the margin there is the note "*Published by Simrock in Berlin 1878*" (in Czech); all this written by Dvořák's own hand.

The manuscript contains the following dates: 1) at the beginning of the first dance "*18 18/3 78*"; 2) after the third dance "*18 4/4 78*"; 3) after the fourth dance "*18 9/4 78*"; 4) after the eighth dance "*V Praze dne 7 máje 1878 | Antonín Dvořák.*" ("Prague May 7th 1878. | Antonín Dvořák.")

The manuscript, very inconsistent as far as dynamic and tempo marks are concerned, was prepared for the engraver with many insertions in pencil and in ink; the insertions in pencil (especially in blue and red pencil) contain many marks concerning the tempo and some concerning the dynamics. Some of these insertions seem to have been written by Dvořák's own hand.

In the manuscript, the dance in A flat major occupies the third place and the dance in D major the sixth place, as also in the orchestral version. This is also how the dances are arranged in the present edition, contrary to Simrock's edition which changed the places of these two dances.

The repetition in the first dance in C major from bar 18 to bar 25 and from bar 171 to bar 178 were inserted by the author additionally, but the corresponding "*II. volta*" was added — obviously by mistake — only in the first case, so that bar 180 contains — also in Simrock's edition — an obvious mistake, the rectification of which, based on the orchestral version, is suggested in the Editorial Notes ("Annotazioni").

In the manuscript the dance in D major continues immediately after bars 1—42 (after which follows the inscription "*von hier aufs Coda*" and the mark ∞) with bars 159*) to

209, i. e. up to the General Pause (which of course made sense only here and not at the end of the dance as it is in the printed edition), then follow bars 43—158, marked in pencil as "*Coda*". After bar 158, with which the manuscript closes, there is the note "*Da Capo* ∞ " which means to continue with bar 159.

The recapitulation of the main part in the dance in G minor is not written out, but only indicated after bar 127 with the words "*Da Capo* ∞ *Coda*", with the mark "*Coda* ∞" after bar 72 and with marking bar 200 as "*Coda*".

b) The printed piano duet edition (N. Simrock, Berlin, 1878).

c) The orchestral version has been consulted only where neither the manuscript nor Simrock's print give an independent and logically satisfactory reading; otherwise both versions differ so often in details as well as in points of purely musical importance that they must be considered as two separate works and it is not possible to regard them as strictly analogous.

Our edition has been based on Simrock's print, published during the composer's lifetime and doubtlessly under his direct supervision. The more important deviations between the sources are listed in the "Annotazioni". Obvious misprints and details omitted in the print have been corrected in accordance with the manuscript. Dynamic marks of minor importance have been added in accordance with analogous passages of both the manuscript and the print. The more important editors' addenda have been put within square brackets.

ABBREVIATIONS:

A = the manuscript of the piano duet version
S = Simrock's edition
SN = the present edition of the State Publishing House KLHU
Orch. = orchestral version
I. = Primo
II. = Secondo
m. d. = right hand
m. s. = left hand
[!] = slip in the manuscript or misprint
Versio I = original version, the change having been carried out by the composer in the manuscript
ex. analog. = corrected in accordance with an analogous place
trad. = usual and accepted way of Czech reproduction

Large Arabic numerals indicate the bar; the small numbers beside them indicate the note (or chord) in the bar; rests are not counted

---

*) bars are numbered correspondingly to the printed edition.

ANNOTAZIONI

1

8 II. m. d. A, S: ; SN ex analog. 55, 161, 208

22–23 II. m. s. A, S: ; SN ex analog.

18–25, 171–178 A Versio I: senza repetizione, senza I^ma volta

66–68 I. m. s. A:

(=64 Versio I); SN =S

100_{1-2} I. m. d. A: ; SN = S

166_1 I. m. s. A, S: [!]?; SN ex analog.

175–180 II. m. s. A, S:

; SN ex analog.

180 I. m. d. A, S: [!]?; SN ossia ex analog.

240 Orch.: tranquillo

2

1 I. m. s. A:*fp* ; S *fp* > ; SN *fp*

2 A Versio I: *Poco allegro*

18 A Versio I:*f*

27–33_1 I. m. s. A:

; SN =S

35_1, 37_1 I. m. s. A: ' ; SN = S

41 I. A, S ʌ̃ ; SN ex analog.

54 A: *Allegretto scherzando. Poco meno, quasi Tempo I.*

63_1, 67_1, 129_1, 133_1 II. m. d. A: ; SN = S

73 II. m. d. A: '' ; SN = S

82 I. A:*ff*; SN = S

110_4 II. m. s. A:*fis*

178, 179 II. A: „Pd"

3

24_4 II. m. s. A: *es* [!] ?; SN = S

49 A: *in Tempo quasi tempo I^mo*

54_4 II. m. s. A [!]; SN = S

70 I. A:*fp*; S:*f*

73 I. II. A:*f*; S: – [!]

82 I. A, S: *p* [!]?

83_1 II. m. d. A, S [!]?; SN ex analog.

96 II. A: *p dimin.*

98 I. A Versio I:*ff pp*

100 I. A, S: *p dimin.*; SN ex analog. 96

101 (105) II. m. d. A: [!]; SN = S

120–121 A: ‖: | :‖ (= 122–123); Orch. senza 122–123

125 I. A: *in tempo* [!]

132_4 I. m. d. A, S [!]; SN ex analog.

186 II. A:*fp*

192 I. II. A, S:*f*; SN ex analog.

195_5 I. m. d. A, S: [!]?; SN ex analog.; (= Orch.)

4

22_4 I. m. d. A, S: [!]?; SN ex analog.

30_{1-3} I. m. d. A: ʌʌʌ ; S: –

48_1 II. m. s. A: (Versio aut.); S: ; SN ex analog.; = A

86 A: I.*f*, II.*ff*; SN = S

95_{4-5} I. m. d. A: [!]; SN = S

133_2 II. A:*f*; SN = S

179 trad.: accelerando sin al 184, 184 ancora più mosso

187 A Versio I:*pp*

182_3, 183_3 I. m. s. A: ; SN = S

5

11_{3-4} I. m. d. A: ; S ; SN ex analog.;

67–68 I. m. s. A:*8^{bassa}*[!]; SN = S   (= Orch.)

75, 77–8 I. II. A, S: senza ♯ (d) [!]; SN ex analog.

81_4 II. m. s. A: [!]; SN = S

125–136 I. m. s. A: etc. simile; SN = S

146 I. m. d. A, S: [!]; SN ex analog. 2/27–33

212 I. m. d. A: [!]; SN = S

217_4, 219_4 I. m. d. A: [!]; SN = S

218_4 I. m. d. A: [!]; SN = S

6

31_5 I. m. d., m. s. A: senza ⌁

35–36 II. m. d. A:  ; SN = S

42 I. m. s. A: ♩ ; SN = S

63_2 I. m. s. A, S: *eis²* [!]?; SN ex analog.; (= Orch.)
68 I. m. d. A, S: ⌁ (senza ♯) [!]; SN ex analog.
75_2 II. m. s. A:*ff*; S: II. *ff*; SN ex analog. I.

115 I. m. d. A: ; SN = S

legato

119_3, 120_3, 121_3 I. m. s. A: ,
129_3 I. m. d. A: >
131–134 I. m. s. A, S: senza ⌒ ; SN ex analog.
182_3 II. m. d. A: (= 4_3 A Versio I); SN = S

202 I. A { m. d.:
      { m. s.:

S m. d. = m. s.:

SN ex analog.; (= Orch.)

7

40 II. m. d. A, S: ʌʌʌʌ ; SN ex analog.
64_4 II. m. d. S: *hes¹* [!]?; SN = A

96_1 II. m. d. A, S: [!]?; SN ex analog.

97_3 I. m. s. A, S: [!]?; SN ex analog.

108–109 I. m. s. A:  [!] (= 106–107

Versio I); SN = S
128 II. m. d. A:*f*; SN = S

143_4 II. m. s. A: [!]; SN = S

187_1 A, S: *Presto*; SN = trad., Orch.

8

1 A Versio I. *Presto*, A: *Allegro vivace*

18_2 (145_2) I. A, S: { [!]?; SN ex analog.

25–32 (152–159) A, S: senza repetizione [!]?; SN ex analog. (= Orch.)
84 trad. più tranquillo

212–213 I. m. s. A, S [!]?; SN ossia

ex analog. 230–231

$229_{2\text{-}3}$ I. m. d. A, S: [!] .; SN ex analog.

239 I. m. d. A: ; SN = S

243 A: „*Majore*"; SN = S
273 A, S: senza ʌ . . . .

Jarmil Burghauser

SLAVONIC DANCES

OP. 72

(Piano duet)

Critical edition based on original sources and prepared for the press by the Editing Board for the Works of Antonín Dvořák': Otakar Šourek, Chairman - Jan Hanuš, Chief Editor - František Bartoš - Dr Jiří Berkovec - Jarmil Burghauser - Dr Antonín Čubr - Ladislav Láska - Antonín Pokorný - Karel Šolc.

TWO SERIES OF "SLAVONIC DANCES", each of them consisting of eight numbers, belong to the most individual, personal and nationally most characteristic and most famous works of *Antonín Dvořák* (8. IX. 1841—1. V. 1904). They were not written successively; the second series (op. 72) followed the first (op. 46) after an interval of eight years. Both series differ substantially in many aspects, but both are typically characteristic of Dvořák not only in construction but also in power of effect and vitality and both originated in the same way. They were written in response to a suggestion of Fritz Simrock, the proprietor of the big publishing house N. Simrock in Berlin. Both were first composed for the piano duet, appeared only later in the full gamour of colourful orchestration and spread quickly throughout the world where time has not only preserved but even heightened their original success.

As soon as Simrock realized the outstanding success of the first series of the "Slavonic Dances" which also proved to be remarkably profitable from the business point of view, he began to urge Dvořák to write a second series. Dvořák at first declined, one reason being that he was at work on large symphonies and oratorios, while another reason was that, with his strong sense of artistic conscienciousness, he was well aware of the seriousness and difficulty of the task of presenting in a new series of "Slavonic Dances" a work which would be really new and whose musical value would not fall below the first which had already won such fame and popularity in the world. In a letter to Simrock (January 1st, 1886) he expressed it in his own way by saying: *"I have to tell you that to do the Slavonic Dances again won't be so easy as it was for the first time. To do the same thing twice is devilishly difficult! As long as I have not the right mood for it, I cannot do it!"* And three days later he again answered an urgent entreaty with the words: *"You imagine composing to be a much simpler process than it really is. One can start only when one feels the proper enthusiasm for the thing!"*

This enthusiasm did, however, come to be felt some five months later and at this time the idea of the new "Slavonic Dances" again captured fully Dvořák's creative imagination. *"Now it goes at full speed"*, he wrote to his publisher at the beginning of June 1886. *"I am enjoying doing the Slavonic Dances immensely and I think they will be altogether different (no joking and no irony)!"* And really—a month later, on July 9th, the manuscript of a new series of eight "Slavonic Dances" for piano duet, bearing the opus number 72, was completed.

Dvořák was right when he wrote that the "Slavonic Dances" of the second series were different from the earlier ones. He not only could not repeat himself, but eight fertile years of artistic development, which also brought about new moods he had not known before, separated him from the first series. If the first series was, in the main, a pure and unaffected manifestation of vitality and gaiety, in the second series this mood, though making itself felt in a number of dances, is in others enveloped to a considerable extent in a veil of poetic meditativeness, and even, as in the fourth dance, yields to a mood of real anguish. Besides, even in the choice of the types of dance Dvořák diverged from the first series. Of the Czech dances introduced earlier he returned only to the "Skočná" ("the Jump Dance", No. 3 of the second series and 11 of the whole cycle), and the "Sousedská" ("Neighbours' Dance", No. 8—16), to which he added the "Špacírka" as he saw it danced by the youth of Vysoká, but for the rest—in addition to two new stylisations of the Ukrainian Dumka (2—10, 4—12) he chose a characteristic Slovak "Odzemek" (1—9), Polish "Mazur" (6—14) and the "Kolo" of the Southern Slavs (7—15). This makes the second series really *Slavonic* in the proper sense of the word. But the touch of genius, the bright and fresh invention and the tremendous extent of the composer's phantasy remained the same as in the first series—or perhaps it was in some places even surpassed.

The second series of the "Slavonic Dances", in its original piano duet version, was published by the Simrock Berlin publishing house at the end of the summer of 1886 and was received with the same enthusiasm as the first. The relation of our first Czech edition to the original Simrock print is discussed in detail in the Editors' Notes following the last page of music.

Translated by Dr L. Dorůžka   Otakar Šourek

EDITORS' NOTES

SOURCES:

a) The manuscript of the original piano version of the second series of the "Slavonic Dances", in the possession of the composer's family, is written rather carelessly but legibly on music paper 308:236 mm in size (after cutting by the book-binder) each page containing 18 staves, and it is bound in a separate volume of 38 sheets. Sheet 31 was faultily bound, its second page (page 6 of the 15th dance) precedig its first page; sheet 32 is not bound but merely inserted. Both these mistakes were caused by the book-binder. The volume has no title page, the first page of the manuscript (which is written in score, i. e. "secondo" under the "primo") bears traces of a piece of paper which was glued on it and again torn off and contains the inscription *"Slovanské tance II | Ant. Dvořák | Vysoká 1886"* ("Slavonic Dances, II."). Besides, there are also some notes for the engraver.

A more accurate title is written at the beginning of the 15th dance as follows: *"Sešit II Zweites Heft | Nro 7. | Slovanské tance | pro piano na čtyři ruce | složil | Ant. Dvořák."* (*"Volume II | No. 7 | Slavonic Dances | for piano duet | composed by | Ant. Dvořák."*) At the end of the last page of the manuscript there is the signature and the date *"Vysoká 9. 7. 1886."*

The manuscript had been prepared for the press very carefully with insertions mostly in red ink (Rob. Keller?) which were additions and adjustments to marks concerning dynamics, phrasing, accidentals and indicated the way the manuscript should be printed. In accordance with the usual practice we consider these insertions as authorised.

The 11th dance contains, after bar 114, six bars which were written out but then cancelled and represented the repeat of bars 67–72; 22 bars were crossed out after bar 134 (answering to bars 21–31 and their further development), and 4 bars were crossed out after bar 138 (development of the preceding bars).

b) The printed piano-duet edition (N. Simrock, Berlin, 1886).

c) The orchestral version which–as it is with the first series–represents an independent work differing in details as well as in important points, was consulted only where neither the manuscript nor the print offered a logically satisfactory reading.

Our edition is based on Simrock's print, published during the composer's lifetime and doubtlessly under his supervision. The more important deviations between the sources are listed in the "Annotazioni". Obvious misprints have been corrected and details omitted in the print have been added in accordance with the manuscript. The missing dynamic marks have been added on the basis of analogous passages of both the manuscript and the print.

ABBREVIATIONS:

A = the manuscript
S = Simrock's edition
SN = the present edition by the State Publishing House KLHU
[!] = slip in the manuscript or misprint
I. = Primo
II. = Secondo
m. d. = right hand
m. s. = left Hand

Orch. = orchestral version
ex analog. = corrected in accordance with an analogous passage
trad. = traditional and accepted way of Czech reproduction

Versio I = the original version, the change having been carried out by the composer in the manuscript

Large Arabic numerals indicate the bar; the small numerals beside them indicate the note (or chord) in the bar; rests are not counted.

ANNOTAZIONI

1 (9)

77 I. A, S ♪. ♫ ♪ ; SN ex analog. 35,202

205₁ II. m. s. S: *E*; SN = A

2 (10)

5₁ II. m. s. S: [!]; SN = A

12 I. m. s. A, S: [!]?; SN ex analog. 28,96 (= Orch.)

19₄ I. A,S: *es²–es³*; SN ex analog. (= Orch.)

3 (11)

25,34 II. m d. A, S : ♪. ♫ ; SN ex analog.

26₁ I. m. d. A,S: *f²* [!]?; SN ex analog.

67–78 I. m. d. S: ⌒⌒⌒…; SN = A

4 (12)

11₃ I. m. s. S, A Versio I. ; SN = A (= 44,89)

23₁₋₂ I. m. d. S: ♪ ♫ [!]; SN = A (= Orch.)

38–39 II. m. s. A, S: ; SN ex analog. (= Orch.)

5 (13)

73 trad.: *poco pesante*

87 II. m. d. A (vers. aut): ; SN = S

87₄ I. m. d. A, S: *cis³*; SN ex analog. 42

6 (14)

98₂ II. m. d. SN= A (S = *f–c₁*)

7 (15)

88 trad. (= Orch.): *poco sosten.*

91 trad. (= Orch.): *in tempo*

Jarmil Burghauser

Complete Slavonic Dances
for Piano Four Hands

Slavonic Dances, Op. 46

1

SECONDO

Slavonic Dances, Op. 46

1

PRIMO

2

2

3

Poco allegro

3

4.4.1878

4

Tempo di minuetto

4

Tempo di minuetto

9. 4. 1878

5

Allegro vivace

5

Allegro vivace

6

Allegretto scherzando

7

Allegro assai

8

8

Presto

Slavonic Dances, Op. 72

SECONDO

1 (9)

Slavonic Dances, Op. 72

PRIMO

1 (9)

2 (10)

2 (10)

3 (11)

3(11)

Un pochettino lento

Un pochettino lento

Tempo I.

Più animato

4 (12)

4 (12)

Allegretto grazioso

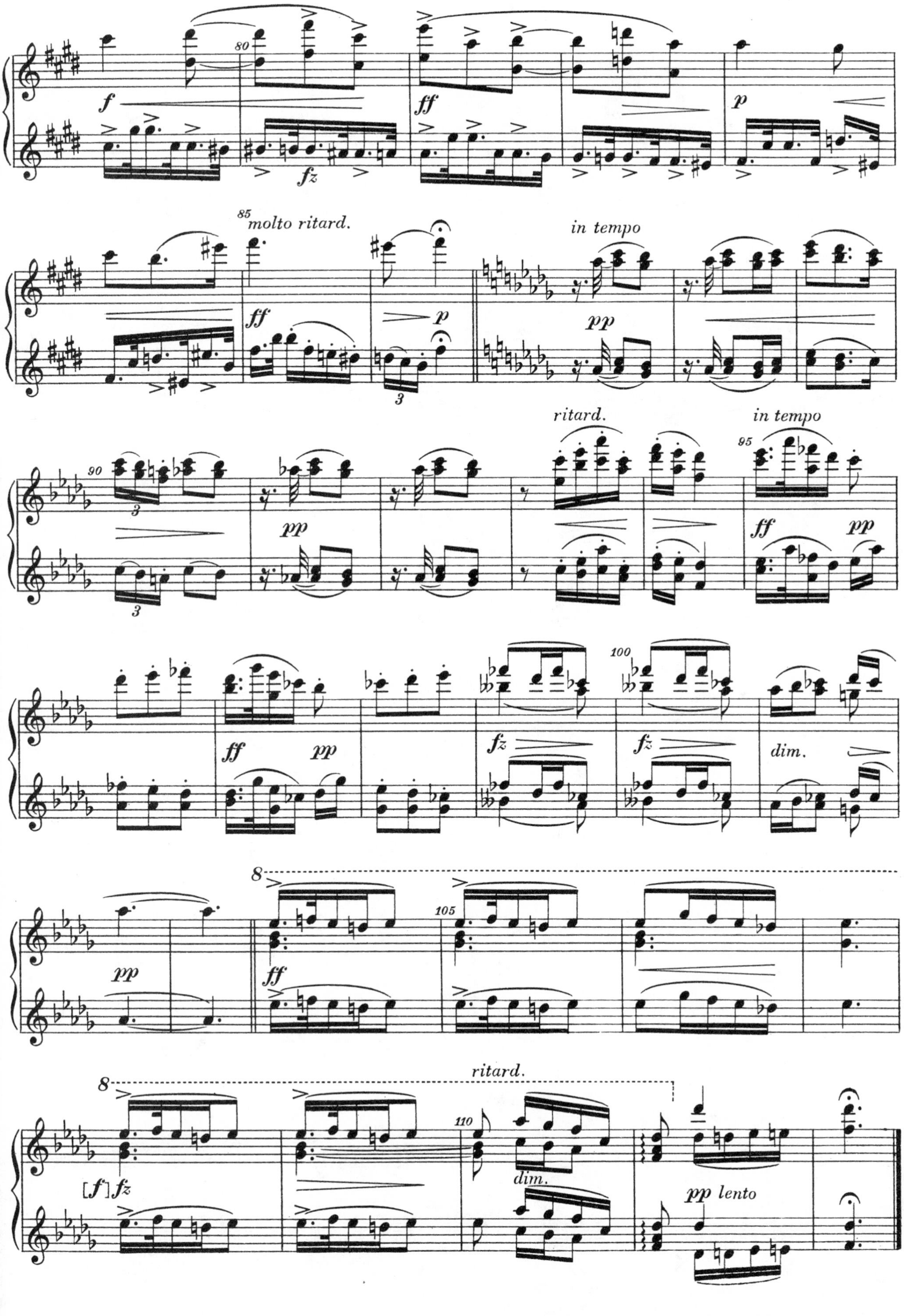
molto ritard.
in tempo
ritard.
in tempo
dim.
dim.
pp lento

5 (13)

5 (13)

SECONDO

6 (14)

Moderato, quasi minuetto

6 (14)

Moderato, quasi minuetto

Un poco più mosso

PRIMO

7 (15)

7 (15)

8 (16)

8 (16)

Lento grazioso, quasi tempo di valse

Vysoká 9.7.1886